FOR JOHN DANIEL AND ALMA MARIE
—S.P. & D.O.

MINEDITIONUS
An imprint of Astra Books for Young Readers, a division of Astra Publishing House
astrapublishinghouse.com
Printed in China

ISBN: 978-1-6626-5097-0 (hc)
ISBN: 978-1-6626-5098-7 (eBook)

Library of Congress Control Number: 2022909169

First edition

10 9 8 7 6 5 4 3 2 1

Design by Ellice M. Lee
The text is set in Recoleta and Lumiere.
Illustrations were done by hand in layers using charcoal, ink, and gouache.

HOW BIRDS SLEEP

BY SARAH PEDRY AND DAVID OBUCHOWSKI

MINEDITIONUS

IT'S DUSK. Unless you're an owl, it's time to get ready for sleep. As the sun goes down, birds all over the world are preparing for a good night's rest.

So how do birds sleep anyway?

BARN OWL, *Tyto alba, United States*

Here, thousands of birds gather to perform an elaborate routine, swirling across the sky like a cloud come to life. These movements are their way of calling other birds from miles away to let them know it's bedtime. When the dance comes to an end, the birds funnel down into the reeds where they will sleep for the night.

TREE SWALLOW, *Tachycineta bicolor, United States*

While some may settle down, others settle up—in the tops of trees, that is. That way, they're out of reach of predators below. Some even sleep stacked, one on top of the other.

GUIRA CUCKOO, *Guira guira, Brazil*

But there's more than one way to sleep on a branch. On cold nights, some birds sleep cuddled together tightly in a snug, warm ball.

LONG-TAILED TIT, *Aegithalos caudatus (europaeus), England*

Others hang upside down.

VERNAL HANGING PARROT, *Loriculus vernalis, Thailand*

In cities where trees are scarce,
billboards, telephone lines, and
rooftops make fine roosts.

It may be loud and bright here, but humans
are mostly harmless compared to the
predators out in the quieter country. And
midnight snacks are always a nice bonus.

ROCK PIGEON, *Columba livia, United States*

Whether it's summer in the desert
or winter in the far north, birds find
nighttime comfort and safety in
unlikely places.

A cactus is prickly but perfect when
it comes to protecting a nest.

CURVE-BILLED THRASHER, *Toxostoma curvirostre, Mexico*

A pillowy-soft snowbank keeps
this bird warm and hidden.

She dives right in!

WILLOW PTARMIGAN, *Lagopus lagopus, Canada*

Far out at sea there's not much to rest on.
Only water and air. That's enough for some birds.

For those with waterproof feathers, the choppy
waves are always at hand to rock them to sleep.

BLACK-LEGGED KITTIWAKE, *Rissa tridactyla, North Atlantic*

SOOTY TERN, *Onychoprion fuscatus, Caribbean Sea*

But birds whose feathers aren't meant to get wet must make their beds in the air. They glide high above the water on warm currents, sleepily flapping their wings just often enough to stay aloft.

Sleeping in the sky may seem strange,
but how about standing on one leg?
As it turns out, that actually helps this
bird stay warm and conserve its energy.

MALLARD, *Anas platyrhynchos, Lebanon*

If you think it's hard getting out from
under your covers in the morning,
imagine waking up as this bird.
It must break free from the ice that
formed around its leg overnight!

ANDEAN FLAMINGO, *Phoenicoparrus andinus, Chile*

Anyway, sleeping on one leg isn't so odd when hundreds of thousands of your friends are doing it, too. During migration, more than half a million of these birds can gather along a single stretch of river. Some take turns watching for predators while the others rest in this marshy oasis.

SANDHILL CRANE, *Antigone canadensis*, *United States*

The largest, strongest, and fastest of the ground birds aren't quite as concerned about predators. They simply sleep out in the open.

COMMON OSTRICH, *Struthio camelus, Kenya*

Domesticated birds, however, aren't so carefree. They prefer a roof over their heads. Walls are nice, too. Inside their coops, safe from hungry predators, young chicks squeeze beneath the wings of their mothers for extra comfort.

DOMESTIC CHICKEN: GOLDEN POLISH, *Gallus gallus domesticus*, *France*

A hanging nest makes a safe and cozy place for this family to sleep. Everyone's happy to stay together, even when fledglings reach adulthood and the next brood arrives.

SOUTHERN PENDULINE TIT, *Anthoscopus minutus, South Africa*

But this little nest only has room for the young.
Their parents make it from leaves still growing
on a branch. They sew the leaves together with
threads of plant fibers, caterpillar
cocoons, or spider silk.

COMMON TAILORBIRD, *Orthotomus sutorius, Hong Kong, China*

Yet some nests are so strong, they can last for generations—even a century. This nest grows larger every day as members of an extended family pitch in, bringing straw to build it bigger.

SOCIABLE WEAVER, *Philetairus socius, Namibia*

Imagine wanting to sleep in a home full of bugs! Well, it's no problem for this bird. After all, the nest belonged to termites in the first place. A bird simply excavated a hole near the top and moved in. Bugs and birds live together in a sturdy shelter made of termite spit and wood pulp.

BUFF-BREASTED PARADISE KINGFISHER, *Tanysiptera sylvia*, *Australia*

At the end of this winding tunnel, birds share a very messy bedroom. Old and young alike sleep soundly amid a mess of undigested bits of insects and seeds.

BLUE-THROATED MOTMOT, *Aspatha gularis*, *Guatemala*

TREE SWALLOW, *Tachycineta bicolor, United States*

Back above ground, darkness fades
and the sun peeks over the horizon.
Birds everywhere begin to stir.

Well, most birds anyway.
Sleep tight, owl.

For everyone else, rise and shine!
The day is here and there's lots to
do before it's time to sleep again.

BARN OWL, *Tyto alba, United States*

WHAT EXACTLY DOES IT MEAN TO BE ASLEEP? For people, sleep is a clearly defined thing. It is a state of rest that can be observed by measuring the activity in the brain. Scientists are able to gauge brain activity by looking at an EEG (electroencephalogram), which shows the brain's electrical signals.

SO WHAT IS SLEEP. ANYWAY?

Of course, your brain is not completely "off" while you sleep. It's still doing important jobs, like keeping your heart beating, your lungs breathing, and your temperature regulated. You also dream when you sleep. Researchers discovered that dreaming occurs during a stage of sleep called REM, which stands for "rapid eye movement." It's called this because, even though your eyes are closed while you're in this stage of sleep, your eyes will move, well, rapidly.

As a species, we humans all sleep in the same general way. But for birds, sleep can look a little different from how it looks for humans. To study how birds sleep, researchers mount small sensors on birds' heads that show them the electrical signals in the birds' brains. These sensors have found a clear difference between the electrical signals that are produced by birds' "awake" brains and their "sleeping" brains. In fact, scientists believe some birds may even dream, as they also have an REM stage of sleep.

But as we've seen in this book, some birds sleep in ways that seem almost impossible. For instance, how is the sooty tern able to sleep while it flies?

The answer lies in the design of the brain. Birds' brains (like our own) are divided into two sides called "hemispheres." With both hemispheres active, the bird (or person) is fully conscious and completely alert. However, birds such as the sooty tern have evolved to be able to sleep with only one hemisphere at a time. With one hemisphere remaining active, there's enough brainpower to keep the bird in flight!

While this may not seem like the most restful way to sleep, it certainly is productive. Adaptations such as these allow birds to migrate, staying safely out of the way of predators or other dangers, all while getting their much-needed rest.

WHEN WE THINK ABOUT climate change, we often think about rising temperatures. But there is much more to the matter than hotter summer days. Climate change means more extreme temperatures in general—colder winters, warmer summers. It also means more frequent, more intense extreme-weather events, such as hurricanes.

In places like the western United States and Australia, summers are becoming more scorching, which increases droughts and wildfire conditions. Coastal areas all over the world are contending with rising sea levels and the flooding that comes with it. Fires and floods are devastating not only to the human population but also to wildlife. These natural disasters destroy habitats, including wiping out the places birds roost. And without sleep, birds, like all creatures, cannot survive.

In areas that are not directly threatened by fire or flood, the climate is still changing. A changing climate can threaten existing plants and animals, which form the ecosystem that animals like birds depend on. Meanwhile, urban sprawl, deforestation, and commercial development of natural landscapes are only making things worse by forcing animals to compete for less space.

It's not too late to make the world a better, healthier place for plants and animals. Here are some things you can do to help birds in particular get a good night's sleep:

Provide structure

What types of structures are best depends on where you live, but it's a good idea to mimic the natural environment. If there are (or were) many trees where you live, some birds in your area will have evolved to roost in trees. So, in this case, try to keep or even plant trees in your yard.

Keep the lights low

Birds don't need a clock to know when it's time for bed, because it's light in the day and dark at night. It's a simple pattern: daylight, dark night, daylight, dark night. But, in populated areas, light pollution can interfere with these natural rhythms (called "circadian rhythms"), confusing birds about where they are and when it's time to rest. If you and your neighbors turn off (or down) your outdoor lights, it can go a long way toward helping birds sleep.

Bring on the baths

Water is a very important part of a bird's habitat. Migrating birds also look for water when they're searching for a place to rest during migration. By providing birdbaths (or natural features that catch and hold water), you're giving feathery friends a place to quench their thirst, cool down, and have a bath—all in view of your window!

THE STORY OF THIS STORY

Birds are everywhere. So whether our family is taking a stroll in a city park or a hike in a national park, we love to do a bit of birding. Our son marvels at majestic raptors, who are always on the hunt for a good meal. Our daughter adores the "poofy" Canada geese that waddle together in their noisy gaggles.

But as much as we love birds, we also love a good mystery. We found exactly that when the question occurred to us: How do birds sleep? We're not the only ones to wonder such a thing. Ornithologists (people who study birds) have long been interested in this subject. Because birds wake easily, can be naturally camouflaged, and sleep in places that are hard to see and sometimes hard to find, it can be quite difficult for researchers to observe and photograph sleeping birds.

In fact, *Birds Asleep* by Alexander F. Skutch (published in 1989 by the University of Texas Press: Austin) is one of the few books dedicated to this topic. We stumbled upon it in a used bookstore one day, and it opened our eyes to just how many different ways and places birds sleep. It also inspired us to not just listen to the birds sing and watch them fly, but also to catch them having a nap.

Now that you've read this book, we hope you'll be inspired to do the same: go outside, listen to the birdsongs, and see them soar. But keep an eye out for telltale signs of birds settling in for a good night (or day) of sleep: a single leg pulled up into the body, a head tucked into a wing, a cozy snuggle on a branch. Once you notice, you'll find it's hard to stop!

—*David Obuchowski & Sarah Pedry*

ACKNOWLEDGMENTS

This book would not have been possible without the inspiration, support, and wisdom of several people. Thank you to Alexander Skutch, Kendra Tyson, E.L., Marc Devokaitis of the Cornell Lab of Ornithology, Dr. Felicity Arengo at the American Museum of Natural History, and Dr. Thomas J. Benson of the Prairie Research Institute at the University of Illinois.

RESOURCES

If you'd like to learn more about birds in your area,
here are some places to start:

The National Audubon Society, audubon.org

The Cornell Lab of Ornithology, birds.cornell.edu/home

National Park Service, nps.gov/index.htm